# LIFESKILLS IN ACTION

## Doing Household Chores

CARRIE
GWYNNE

# LIFESKILLS IN ACTION

## LIVING SKILLS

**MONEY**

Living on a Budget | Road Trip
Opening a Bank Account | The Guitar
Managing Credit | High Cost
Using Coupons | Get the Deal
Planning to Save | Something Big

**LIVING**

Smart Grocery Shopping | Shop Smart
Doing Household Chores | Keep It Clean
Finding a Place to Live | A Place of Our Own
Moving In | Pack Up
Cooking Your Own Meals | Dinner Is Served

**JOB**

Preparing a Résumé
Finding a Job
Job Interview Basics
How to Act Right on the Job
Employee Rights

SADDLEBACK
EDUCATIONAL PUBLISHING
www.sdlback.com

All source images from Shutterstock.com

ISBN-13: 978-1-68021-040-8
ISBN-10: 1-68021-040-8
eBook: 978-1-63078-346-4

Printed in Guangzhou, China
NOR/0116/CA21600020

20 19 18 17 16    1 2 3 4 5

**Household chores**.

We do them to make our homes clean.

Wash clothes. Mop floors. Clean rooms.

Keep them neat and tidy.

Cleaning is just one part of chores.

**Upkeep** is important too.

Hang a picture. Change a lightbulb. Fix a leak.

We take care of our homes.

It is all part of living clean.

We want to live healthy too.

Chores help us do this.

But they take time.

What happens if we wait?

Things get out of hand.

Avoid this by staying **organized**.

Manage your time.

Find a way to fit it all in.

It helps to do a few chores each day.

And it's worth it.

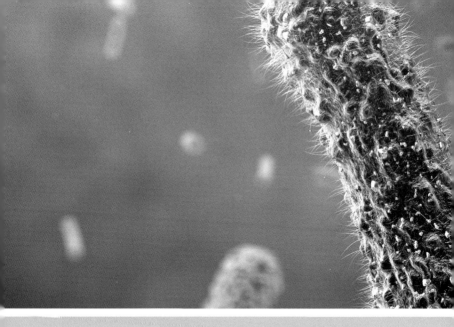

Doing chores is good for your health.

Cleaning kills germs.

There is less of the **bacteria** that can make you ill.

A tidy home saves you time too.

Things are easy to find.

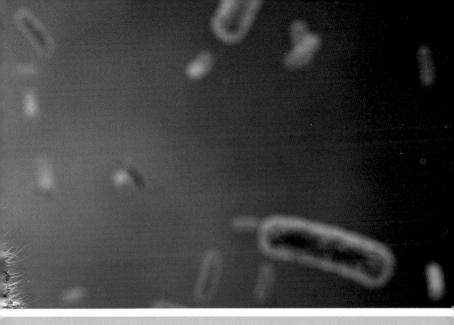

We all like to save money.

Chores help with this too.

Things last longer when
you take care of them.

Rugs. Floors.
Blinds.

It pays to live
clean.

How do you start?

**Make a list**.

Put the chores in order.

Daily and weekly chores go first.

Do the laundry.

Clean the kitchen and the bathroom.

Take out the trash.

Then list repairs and upkeep.

Fill a nail hole. Paint a wall.

Clean up after pets.

Next are chores that help things look tidy.

Make the bed.

Pick up clutter.

Put things away.

Monthly chores go last.

You do these less often.

But they are just as important.

Pay the bills.

Clean out the closet.

Dust the blinds.

| SUN | MON | TUE | |
|---|---|---|---|
| 01 | 02<br>TAKE TRASH<br>TO CURB | 03 | LA |
| 08<br>PLAN MEALS<br>SHOP | 09<br>TAKE TRASH<br>TO CURB | 10 | |
| 15 | 16<br>TAKE TRASH<br>TO CURB | 17 | LA |
| 22<br>PLAN MEALS<br>SHOP | 23<br>TAKE TRASH<br>TO CURB | 24 | |
| 29 | 30<br>TAKE TRASH<br>TO CURB | 31<br>WASH<br>WINDOWS | |

Now make a **schedule**.

Use a calendar or make a chart.

Fill in the chores.

Divide them up.

Daily. Weekly. One time each month.

This is your cleaning plan.

Try to follow it.

Other things may come up.

It may be hard to fit it all in.

Saving time is easy.

Clean smart.

How? Here are some ways.

# Be prepared.

Have the right products and tools on hand.

## Tools and Cleaning Products

### Tools:

- vacuum
- broom
- mop
- paper towels
- sponges
- rubber gloves

### Cleaning Products:

- all-purpose cleaner
- dish soap
- laundry detergent
- dishwasher detergent
- disinfectant (germ killer)
- bleach
- ammonia
- wood cleaner for wood floors
- cleaner for a stainless steel refrigerator
- window cleaner
- carpet cleaner
- oven cleaner

**Choose carefully**.

Look at each bottle.

Read the label on the back.

It tells you what the product does.

Learn how to use it safely.

Do not mix cleaners.

This is dangerous.

Use them one at a time.

**Get organized**.

Put cleaning products in bins.

Have a bin for each room.

**Clean as you go**.

Tidy a room as you walk through it.

Pick up the clutter. Put items back in place.

Wipe the counter and mirror when you are in the bathroom.

Clean the kitchen as you cook.

Wash the dishes after you eat.

**Do not overload yourself**.

Some chores are a big job.

Cleaning the bathroom is one of them.

But it doesn't have to take hours.

Do a **basic clean** a few times a week.

Counter. Sink. Toilet. Tub.

Or clean it once a week.

Do a **deep clean**.

This is more than the basics.

Clean the room from top to bottom.

Cabinets. Walls. Baseboards and floors.

**Be a dirt detective**.

Some problems in a home can hide.

Know where to look and what to look for.

**Cobwebs**.

They form on the ceiling and in the corners.

**Soap scum**.

It coats the shower walls and doors.

**Mold**.

It can grow in wet areas. Check the shower and under sinks.

**A bad odor**.

It may be coming from the garbage disposal.

Pieces of food may be stuck there.

Or there may be old food in the refrigerator.

**Grease**.

It can build up where you cook.

Check around the stove. Cabinets. Wall.

Don't wait until you have problems.

Try to **prevent** them.

A house. An apartment. A rented room.

Wherever you live, most chores are the same.

Keep the inside clean and tidy.

Maintain your home too.

Decorate. Make small repairs.

Some tasks are simple.

But they keep you healthy and safe.

Check air filters.

Change them when they are full of dust and dirt.

Test the battery in the smoke alarm.

Change it two times a year.

Use a mold cleaner in rooms with wet areas.

Keep your home in **good condition**.

Fill a nail hole when you take down a picture.

Touch up a scratch in the paint.

Wipe up a spill as soon as it happens.

Clean up after pets.

Make sure that a stain does not sit.

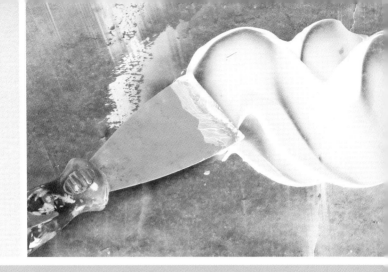

The longer it sits, the harder it is to get out.

It looks bad.

And cleaning it is cheaper than buying a new rug.

There are less chores in an apartment.

Apartments have **managers**.

They do many jobs.

Take care of the trash and the yard.

Fix things that are broken or not working.

Make things safe.


Houses do not have a manager.

You are **responsible** for the chores.

Inside and outside.

Mow the lawn.

Take the trash bins out to the curb.

Bring them back in.

Clean the garage.

Make sure it is neat and safe.

Store things in boxes.

Keep tools in one place.

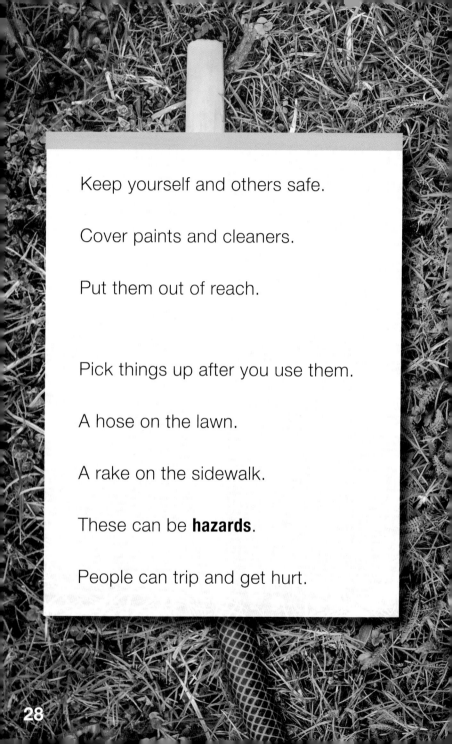

Keep yourself and others safe.

Cover paints and cleaners.

Put them out of reach.


Pick things up after you use them.

A hose on the lawn.

A rake on the sidewalk.

These can be **hazards**.

People can trip and get hurt.

Make things neat.

Sweep the porch.

Shake out the doormat.

Dust the lights.


Your home will be safe.

It will look good too.

**Doing chores**.

It takes a lot of work.

But your home will be clean.

You will be healthy too.

That can make everything in your life better.

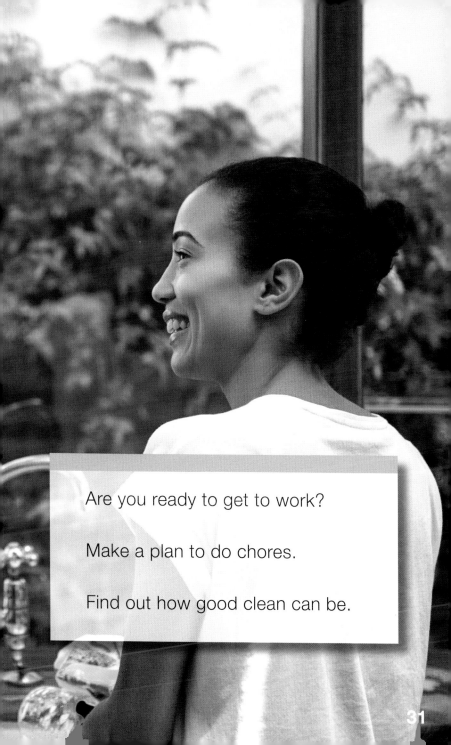

Are you ready to get to work?

Make a plan to do chores.

Find out how good clean can be.

What happens when a person does not keep up with chores? That is what Jake finds out in *Keep It Clean*. Want to read on?

KEEP IT CLEAN

PJ GRAY

JUST *flip* THE BOOK!

PJ GRAY

KEEP IT
CLEAN

# LIFESKILLS IN ACTION

## SADDLEBACK
EDUCATIONAL PUBLISHING
www.sdlback.com

All source images from Shutterstock.com

ISBN-13: 978-1-68021-040-8
ISBN-10: 1-68021-040-8
eBook: 978-1-63078-346-4

Printed in Guangzhou, China
NOR/0116/CA21600020

20 19 18 17 16   1 2 3 4 5

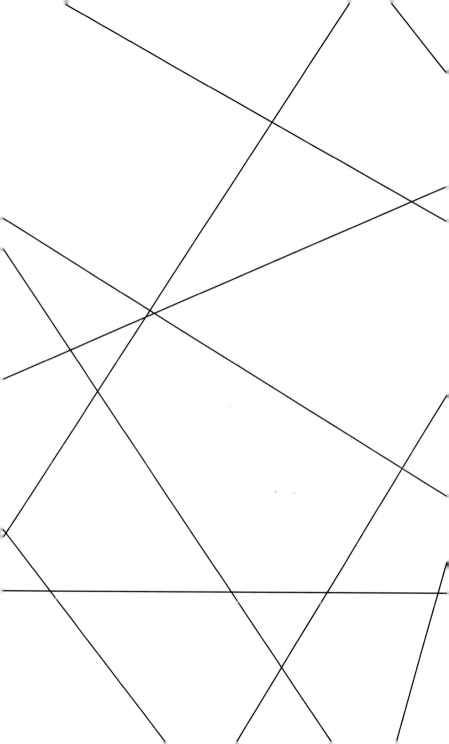

Jake Jones was a senior. He kept busy.

First there was football. Jake was a
linebacker. Then there were his friends.
Some were on the team with him. Others
he had hung out with for years.

Most of all there was his car. It was new.
Jake was so proud of it. He washed it
twice a week. And he liked to show it off.

Jake lived with his mom. His mom sold cars for a living. She worked long hours.

Mrs. Jones made a deal with Jake. She would do part of the chores.

"I will cook and shop for groceries," said his mom. "And I will wash clothes and dust the house. Keeping my room and bathroom clean will be my job. But you need to do your part too."

Jake agreed. "Okay. What do you need me to do?"

His mom smiled. "You can wash the dishes. Take out the trash, and put the bins out once a week. Mow the yard. And keep your room and bathroom clean."

They shook hands. It was a deal.

Mrs. Jones was proud of her son. She loved him very much. But she had one problem. Jake would not do his chores.

One day Mrs. Jones came home from work. She had been grocery shopping. There was a back door into the kitchen. Mrs. Jones went there with the groceries. Then she stopped.

What a mess! Three trash bags were outside the door. Jake never put them into the bin.

One bag was ripped open. The dog next door must have done it. Old food and trash were in the backyard. The back gate was open. Jake had not locked it.

Mrs. Jones was mad. She called Jake. But he did not pick up.

She sent him a text. "Where are you?"

"Car wash," he texted back.

"Please come home now," she texted. "BIG mess in backyard."

"Will clean later. Going to the movies."

Mrs. Jones shook her head. But she was tired. She went inside and put away the groceries.

One day Mrs. Jones came home from work. She got out of her car.

The front yard looked bad. The grass was very high. Jake had not mowed it. She had asked him many times. Jake said that he would do it. But he never did.

Mrs. Jones pulled out her phone. She sent a text to Jake. "You did not cut the grass. You said you would."

Jake sent back a text. "Will do later."

"You keep saying that," she texted back. "You promised last week."

They ate dinner that night.

"Thanks for dinner, Mom," Jake said.

Jake's cell rang. He got up from the table.

"Hold on," Mrs. Jones said. "We need to talk."

"Okay," Jake said, looking at his phone.

"Look at all the dirty dishes. You have a job to do."

Jake looked at the dishes in the sink. "Can you do them this time?" Jake asked. "I've got a ton of homework."

"It will only take a few minutes."

"Please, Mom," Jake said.

"You have not done dishes all week."

"Please, Mom! Thanks."

Jake took his phone. He went upstairs to his bedroom.

Mrs. Jones washed the dishes. Then she went upstairs to Jake's room. His door was ajar. She could hear him talking. Jake was still on his phone.

"Hang up," Mrs. Jones said. "Hang up right now."

Jake hung up his phone. "I'm doing my homework," he said.

"It doesn't sound like it."

"I am. I swear I am," he said.

Mrs. Jones looked at Jake's room. Dirty clothes were on the floor. His bed was not made. Books and papers were thrown about.

"Your room is a mess," she said. "I asked you to keep it clean."

"I've been very busy," Jake said.

"What is that smell? Something is rotten in here."

"Don't worry," Jake said. "I will clean it. I promise."

"You keep saying that. And what about the trash? You still need to take that out."

"I will," Jake said.

"I've been doing it for you all week. It only takes a few minutes."

"I will, Mom. I promise."

"Don't forget the bin," Mrs. Jones said.

"What bin?" Jake asked.

"The trash bin!" she replied. "Make sure the bags go into the bin."

"I do that," he said. "Who says that I don't?"

"The dog next door," she said.

Mrs. Jones turned and walked across the hall. She stepped into Jake's bathroom. It was a mess.

Bath towels were on the floor. The sink was dirty. The bathtub had mildew growing in it.

Mrs. Jones shook her head. She walked back to Jake's bedroom. "Your bathroom is dirty," she said to Jake.

"I will clean it," he said.

"When?"

"When I clean my bedroom," Jake said. "I clean them at the same time. I will clean them. I promise."

Mrs. Jones turned to leave. "Hey, Mom," Jake said. "I won't be home until late on Friday."

"Why?"

"I've got a date," Jake said. "I will pick her up after football practice."

"Who is she?" Mrs. Jones asked.

"Her name is Kim. She's nice. You would like her. She's the best-looking girl in school. I have asked her out all year. She finally said yes."

Friday night came. Mrs. Jones got home from work. Jake was still at football practice.

Mrs. Jones looked in Jake's room. He had never cleaned it. It was still a big mess. And it smelled bad.

She looked in Jake's bathroom. He had never cleaned it. It was a mess. Mrs. Jones was mad. Very mad.

The doorbell rang. There was a pretty girl at the door. Mrs. Jones smiled.

"Hi," the girl said. "Is Jake here?"

"Are you Kim?" Mrs. Jones asked.

"Yes."

"Please come on in," she said. "I'm Jake's mom."

Kim stepped into the living room. "Would you like something to drink?" Mrs. Jones asked.

"No, thank you," Kim said.

"Jake is not here."

"I know," Kim said. "He was going to pick me up. I just sent him a text. I told him I would meet him here instead. I only live a block away."

"I see," Mrs. Jones said. She then looked upstairs. "Jake should be here very soon. Make yourself at home. Would you like to wait in his room?"

Kim looked at Mrs. Jones. "His bedroom? Really? Are you sure?"

"Sure. I'm a cool mom," she said. "Jake is very proud of his room. It's just up the stairs. First door on the left."

"Okay, thanks," Kim said. "May I use your bathroom first?"

"Yes," Mrs. Jones said. "The bathroom is upstairs. First door on the right. Across from Jake's room."

Kim walked up the stairs. Mrs. Jones heard her open the bathroom door. Then she heard a gasp.

A few seconds went by. Then she heard Kim walk into Jake's bedroom.

Mrs. Jones heard a car outside. She looked out the window. It was Jake. He got out of the car. Then he ran through the tall grass.

The front door blew open. Jake jumped through the doorway. "Where is she?" Jake asked.

"Who?" his mom asked.

"Kim! My date! She sent me a text. She said she was coming here."

"Kim?" Mrs. Jones asked. "Oh, Kim. Yes, I met her. You were right. She is very nice."

"Where is she?" Jake asked.

"Your date went up to your room. Your clean room," Mrs. Jones said.

"Wait," Jake said. "My room? Kim did what?"

"She is up there right now."

Jake's eyes opened wide. "MOM! NO!"

He ran up the stairs.

# JUST *flip* THE BOOK!

CARRIE GWYNNE

LIVING SKILLS+

Doing Household Chores

LIFESKILLS IN ACTION

How could Jake have avoided the mess he got into? Want to learn more about how cleaning smart can lead to a healthier life?